3/11

SPORTS HEROES
of Ancient Greece

Paul Mason

Crabtree Publishing Company

www.crabtreebooks.com

Author: Paul Mason
Editor: Kathy Middleton
Production coordinator: Ken Wright
Prepress technician: Margaret Amy Salter
Series consultant: Gill Matthews

Picture Credits:
Alamy Images: Ace Stock Ltd 7b, 21, 28,
  Andrea Matone 22
Fotolia: Ikthus2010 25l
Photolibrary: 8, View Stock 14
Shutterstock: (Cover) Mark Higgins, Murat Besler 10,
  Brendan Howard 25r, Elpis Ioannidis 7t, Panos
  Karapanagiotis 29b, Georgios Kollidas 24, Mike
  Liu 6, Timothy R. Nichols 4, 29t, Phy 5b, 9b, 20,
  Carmen Ruiz 13, Jozef Sedmak 26, Topal 9t,
  Uran92 5t
Wikimedia Commons: 16, 19, Marie-Lan Nguyen 17,
  Bibi Saint-Pol 27
Illustrations: Pippa Cornell and Geoff Ward

Every effort has been made to trace copyright holders and to obtain their permission for use of copyright material. The authors and publishers would be pleased to rectify any error or omission in future editions. All the Internet addresses given in this book were correct at the time of going to press. The author and publishers regret any inconvenience caused if addresses have changed or sites have ceased to exist, but can accept no responsibility for any such changes.

Library and Archives Canada Cataloguing in Publication

Mason, Paul, 1967-
    Sports heroes of ancient Greece / Paul Mason.

(Crabtree connections)
Includes index.
ISBN 978-0-7787-9911-5 (bound).--ISBN 978-0-7787-9932-0 (pbk.)

    1. Athletics--Greece--History--To 1500--Juvenile literature.
2. Athletes--Greece--History--To 1500--Juvenile literature.
3. Olympic games (Ancient)--Juvenile literature. 4. Sports--
Greece--History--To 1500--Juvenile literature. I. Title.
II. Series: Crabtree connections

GV21.M38 2011   j796.0938   C2010-905072-X

Library of Congress Cataloging-in-Publication Data

Mason, Paul.
    Sports heroes of ancient Greece / Paul Mason.
       p. cm. -- (Crabtree connections)
Includes index.
    ISBN 978-0-7787-9932-0 (pbk. : alk. paper) -- ISBN 978-0-7787-9911-5
(reinforced library binding : alk. paper)
    1. Athletics--Greece--History--To 1500--Juvenile literature. 2.
Athletes--Greece--History--To 1500--Juvenile literature. 3. Olympic
games (Ancient)--Juvenile literature. 4. Sports--Greece--History--To
1500--Juvenile literature. I. Title.
    GV21.M37 2011
    796.0938--dc22
                                    2010030822

Crabtree Publishing Company

www.crabtreebooks.com   1-800-387-7650

Printed in the U.S.A./082010/WO20101210

Published in Canada
Crabtree Publishing
616 Welland Ave.
St. Catharines, Ontario
L2M 5V6

Published in the United States
Crabtree Publishing
PMB 59051
350 Fifth Avenue, 59th Floor
New York, New York 10118

CONTENTS

SPORTS HEROES

I am Adrastos, the greatest trainer in all of Greece!

It's great being a sports hero— who *wouldn't* want to be one? Olympic champions are among the most respected people here in Greece.

These two athletes are hoping to wrestle their way to Olympic glory.

Big-time rewards!

Everybody knows about the big-time rewards that come from being a sports hero. You are showered with glory. Money, houses, free meals for life, and all sorts of other treats come your way.

Taking on the challenge

Of course, it's not easy to become an Olympic hero. "Adrastos!" the young boys say to me. "It's such a lot of work." Well, anything worth having is hard to get! But maybe the hard work is why there are fewer youngsters at my coaching school these days.

Perhaps this book will persuade a few more promising athletes to take up the challenge.

This young athlete from a rival school is training for the discus.

OLYMPIC EVENTS

There's an event for everyone:
- horse racing and chariot racing
- combat sports—boxing, wrestling, and *pankration*
- running—various distances
- pentathlon—discus, javelin, long jump, running, and wrestling

Find out more about Olympic events on page 30.

ASTYLOS OF CROTON

Some people might say that training to be
an Olympic hero is tough but just think of
the rewards. Remember the story of one of the
best-rewarded Olympians ever, Astylos of Croton?

At the race track at
Olympia, Astylos raced the
stadion (one length of the track)
and diaulos (two lengths).

Running after the money

In 488 BC, Astylos ran for his home city, Croton. When he won, the **citizens** were so pleased they put up a giant statue of him and gave him a house. Imagine!

Of course, the story of Astylos's riches doesn't end there. The people of the **city-state** of Syracuse offered Astylos even more to run for *them*. Greedy Astylos changed cities.

The people of Croton were very annoyed. They knocked down their statue of Astylos and turned his old house into the local jail. Astylos didn't care—he was enjoying life in Syracuse.

How great would it be if your town put up a statue in honor of your victory?

VICTORY WREATHS

Winners of athletic competitions in ancient Greece are rewarded with victory **wreaths**. Olympic wreaths are always made of olive branches.

Everyone agrees that Astylos was the best runner the Olympics ever saw. He won six victory wreaths at three different Games.

GOT WHAT IT TAKES?

No one says winning at the Olympics is easy. Some people say that all the hard work isn't worth it. Ridiculous! What do they know? Yes, you might fail. But succeed, and you'll be famous forever.

You'll need to put in hours of training, but the rewards are worth it.

Starting young

Let's assume you're a brave young man, not a shivering coward afraid to take risks. Where do you start? The route to the Games starts young—so far, the youngest champion was only 12.

REASONS TO ENTER THE OLYMPICS

- To prove to yourself you can do it
- Fame (including a statue of yourself in your town square, if you're lucky)
- Money—not that you'll need it, because you'll be getting:
  1. free meals for life;
  2. a free house to live in;
  3. free clothes;
  4. free just about everything else.

Get the best trainer

The most promising young athletes work with a trainer like me. We trainers are expensive! But if you can't afford one, maybe your city will pay. In return, we make sure you eat the right foods, provide **massages**, and train you in your special event.

We trainers help our athletes to improve—even if it means a poke with a sharp stick every now and again!

DID YOU KNOW?

Greek athletes often exercise to flute music. This helps them perform gracefully.

SPORTS— NOT WAR

The Olympics isn't only a good thing for the athletes and **spectators**. It is also good for the rest of Greece. Why? Because the Games bring a bit of peace to the war-like Greek world!

> We Greeks are always at war over something. The only thing that ever stops us from fighting is the Olympics.

There's always something

Everyone knows what Greeks are like. There's always something to fight about. If it's not wars between cities, it's brawls in the **taverna** or arguments in the town square. All this fighting makes traveling from one side of Greece to the other a dangerous thing.

The Olympic truce

The Olympics are important to people everywhere. They are so important that we stop our wars to let travelers reach the Games. We call this the "Olympic truce." It starts a month before the Games begin.

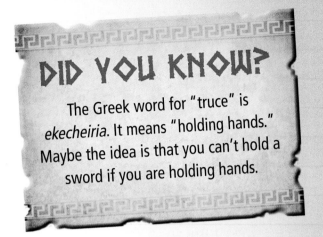

DID YOU KNOW?

The Greek word for "truce" is *ekecheiria*. It means "holding hands." Maybe the idea is that you can't hold a sword if you are holding hands.

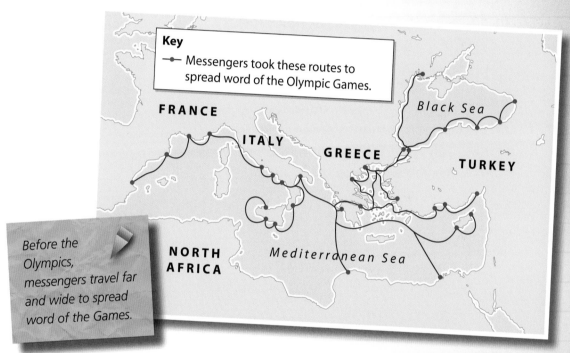

Key

— Messengers took these routes to spread word of the Olympic Games.

FRANCE

ITALY

GREECE

Black Sea

TURKEY

NORTH AFRICA

Mediterranean Sea

Before the Olympics, messengers travel far and wide to spread word of the Games.

BAAA-BARIANS!

When the Lacedaemonians (Las-ee-day-moan-ee-ans) broke the Olympic truce, they were banned from the Games. They were also fined 2,000 *minae*—the equivalent to the cost of 20,000 sheep—for being such **barbarians**!

FRIENDS AND RIVALS

A month before the Games, athletes from all over the Greek-speaking world arrive. Everyone takes their training seriously, but you'll still find time to have fun.

City competitors

We Greeks have cities all round the Mediterranean. Athletes arrive from southern France, Italy, Egypt, Libya, and even as far as Tunisia, as well as Greece itself, of course.

Athletes traveled from every place on this map to compete in the Olympic Games at Olympia.

Rivals and friends

Obviously, some of the other athletes will be your **rivals** when the Games start—but most won't. Think of the fun you'll have meeting runners, wrestlers, boxers, charioteers, horsemen, and everyone else.

There are important people at the Games, too—leaders and great men from all the main Greek cities. Who knows? One of them might decide to become your supporter, helping you out with money and other benefits. You'd be set for life.

These days, athletes must compete naked. That's one way to make sure women can't sneak in!

NO WOMEN ALLOWED!

There are no female athletes at the Games. That would be completely unsuitable! We Greeks know that women should stay at home and look after their children. Young girls and unmarried women can come to the Games—as long as a man supervises them to make sure they don't peek at the athletes!

13

HANGING OUT

As an athlete, you wouldn't have to rub shoulders with the ordinary people at the Games. And it's a good thing, too—over 40,000 of them come. Most have to camp, packed tightly together in the fields and woods nearby.

I feel a bit of healthy competition in the gym always helps improve training.

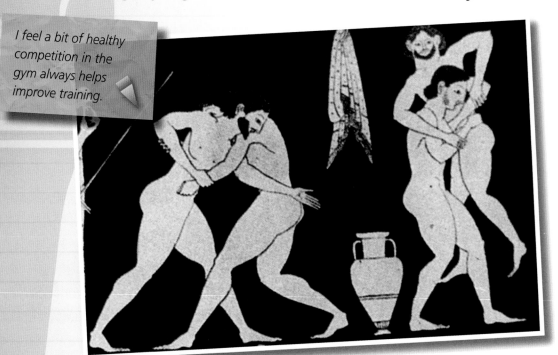

Special lodgings, sir?

Inside the Olympic grounds, there's special accommodation set aside for athletes. It is right next to the *gymnasion*, where you'd be practicing in the month leading up to the Games. The only other people who get to stay inside the Olympic site are priests and the most important **dignitaries**.

❶ Running track,
   or *stadion*

❷ Horse track,
   or *hippodrome*

❸ Training complex,
   or *gymnasion*

❹ Wrestling grounds,
   or *palaistra*

❺ Baths

❻ Council house

This map of the Olympic
site will help you find
your way around. There
are some parts where only
athletes are allowed, of course.

Athletes only!

TOUGH MAN

How would you like to be famous as the toughest man alive? If you win at *pankration*, that's just what you'd be! *Pankration* is my old event. In fact, I am named after a brave, fierce Greek king called Adrastos. I was always brave in *pankration*—even when someone was trying to break my fingers!

The judges watch a pankration *bout. I was never sure why we needed judges. There are only two rules.*

No-limits fighting!

Pankration is real no-limits fighting. There's no time limit. There's no weight limit, and there are only two rules. The main aim is to overpower your opponent—by whatever means.

Some say that because fighters can't be **prosecuted** if their opponent is killed, the game is too dangerous. But imagine how you'd feel if you won!

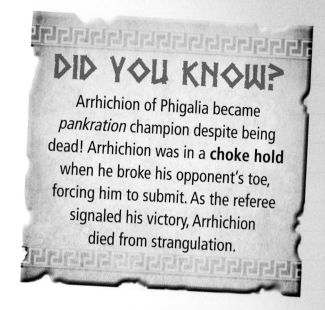

DID YOU KNOW?

Arrhichion of Phigalia became *pankration* champion despite being dead! Arrhichion was in a **choke hold** when he broke his opponent's toe, forcing him to submit. As the referee signaled his victory, Arrhichion died from strangulation.

PANKRATION RULES

There are only two rules in *pankration*:
1. You can't bite.
2. You can't try to pluck out the other fighter's eyes.

So, that means you can do any of the following:

- kick
- punch
- knee
- elbow
- throw
- crush
- break
- twist

Look at these two! The bent-over one is biting. That's breaking the rules!

MILO OF CROTON

If you need encouragement when training gets tough, look no further than the biggest Olympic hero of them all—six-time wrestling champion Milo of Croton.

Growing stronger every day

Milo built up his strength from a very young age in an unusual way. He carried a calf around every day! Think of that if you feel faint-hearted during training.

ITALY

• Croton

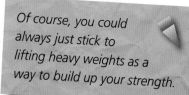

Of course, you could always just stick to lifting heavy weights as a way to build up your strength.

Milo came from Croton, in southern Italy.

Legendary champion

Milo first won at the Olympics in the boys' wrestling contest. Eight years later he came back and won the first of five men's wreaths. Milo was only finally defeated at his seventh Games. That kind of glory could be yours too, with a little effort.

THE STRONGEST MAN IN GREECE

To show his strength, Milo would hold a ripe pomegranate in his fist and challenge people to take it from him. No one ever managed to peel back even a finger, and the pomegranate was never even bruised.

DID YOU KNOW?

Walking in the woods, Milo spotted a tree trunk split with wedges. He decided to see if he could pull the trunk apart. When he tried, it snapped shut, trapping his hands. Milo was then eaten alive by wild animals.

NOT a nice way to go— eaten alive with your hand trapped in a tree. Ouch!

GREEK HERO

Everyone agrees that Olympic champions are the finest men anywhere in Greece. In fact, we all say they are as close to the legendary Greek heroes as men can be.

Here are two Olympians boxing. Now, that's how it should be done. A fine example!

Be the best!

Becoming Olympic champion is great. It is one of the few ways that ordinary people can reach the very top of Greek society. Once you are there, you will be respected by everyone. People will say of you, "He's honest and fair and the absolute best at what he does." Who wouldn't want that?

Imagine a boxer you can't hit! That was Melankomas of Karia, one of the greatest boxers ever.

Hit or miss

Melankomas of Karia was one Greek who certainly showed *arete* (to be the best). First he decided life in the army would be too easy and became a boxer instead. Then he won his fights by being impossible to hit. He didn't hit his opponents—he wore them out by making them miss.

CHEATS BEWARE!

Sadly, a few athletes have let the Games down. Here are a couple of names that still make people shake their heads in disgust:

- Eupolus of Thessaly, who bribed other boxers to let him win
- Callippus of Athens (lying Athenians!), who paid other **pentathletes** to lose

DIAGORAS OF RHODES

No Greek athlete was ever more admired than Olympic champion Diagoras of Rhodes. He is an example not only to Olympic athletes, but to us all.

This famous statue shows Diagoras being carried into the Olympic arena by his sons, who were also Olympic champions.

TURKEY

Rhodes

Diagoras came from the island of Rhodes.

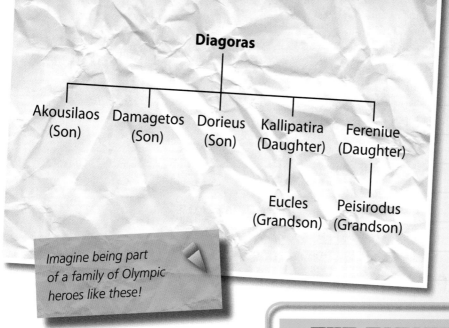

Diagoras
- Akousilaos (Son)
- Damagetos (Son)
- Dorieus (Son)
- Kallipatira (Daughter)
  - Eucles (Grandson)
- Fereniue (Daughter)
  - Peisirodus (Grandson)

Imagine being part of a family of Olympic heroes like these!

A great boxer

When Diagoras won the Olympic boxing wreath in 464 BC, no one was surprised. After all, this was the boxer who once recorded a perfect season, winning all four of the big Games in Greece in one year.

A great man

People did not only admire Diagoras for his sports skills. They also admired him because he was **modest**, honest, and open. People say Diagoras even refused to avoid other fighters' blows. He thought it was too much like cheating.

THE TOUGHEST FAMILY IN GREECE!

This is one family you don't want to pick a fight with! Diagoras, his sons, and grandsons won enough Olympic olive wreaths to plant their own olive grove.

Diagoras—Olympic boxing champion

His sons:
Damagetos—twice Olympic *pankration* champion
Akousilaos—Olympic boxing champion
Dorieus—three times Olympic *pankration* champion

His grandsons:
Eucles (son of Kallipatira (see page 27)) —Olympic boxing champion
Peisirodus—boys' Olympic boxing champion

23

FOR THE GODS

By now, you must have found plenty of reasons to want to be an Olympic champion. But the most important of all is still to come—honoring the gods. In particular, honoring Zeus, the ruler of the gods.

Zeus's games

The whole Games are dedicated to Zeus.
- On the first day, the athletes swear the Olympic Oath in front of a giant statue of Zeus.
- On the third day, a huge procession is held in his honor. A hundred oxen are **sacrificed**.
- On the final, fifth day, the winners are given their prizes at the Temple of Zeus.

Zeus was the most important of all the ancient Greek gods.

Zeus only throws thunderbolts at losers. Just make sure you win.

Getting closer to the gods

Winning the Olympics is the closest a **mortal** man can get to the gods. Don't forget, the Olympics share their name with Mount Olympus, where the gods live.

Some people even claim that Olympic winners are descended from gods. The people of Rhodes are always saying that Diagoras is descended from the god Hermes.

Mount Olympus is the home of the Gods.

Perhaps Diagoras did descend from the Greek god Hermes (left).

JUST FOR WOMEN

Some people say there's not much for women at the Games. Nonsense! Why, there are even female Olympic champions. But how can that be, when married women can't even go as spectators?

In equestrian events, if a woman owns the horse she is named the winner.

The first woman to win

The first woman to be listed as Olympic champion was Kyniska of Sparta. At the Games, it is the owners of horses who win **equestrian** events, not the riders or drivers. Kyniska's four-horse chariot won at two Olympics in a row.

Games—for women!

There are games especially for women at the Olympic site. We men don't know much about them—only women are allowed. They are on a different date from the men's Games, of course! The women's games are called the *Heraia* and are held every four years. The *Heraia* honors the goddess Hera, wife of Zeus.

Here is Hera, the beautiful wife of Zeus. (She's the one on the left.)

DID YOU KNOW?

One woman, Kallipatira, sneaked into the Games dressed as a man. She wanted to watch her son Eucles box. When Kallipatira leaped over a barrier to congratulate Eucles on winning, her secret was found out. As her clothes flew up in the air, it became obvious she wasn't a man!

Fortunately for Kallipatira, her father, husband, and son were all famous Olympic winners, so the judges decided to let her off easy.

WHEN CAN YOU START?

There are very few boys like the great runner, boxer, and *pankratist* Theagenes. His strength and boldness made him a legend by the time he was nine! And he hadn't even won an Olympic event yet. Get the right coaching, and you too could be a hero just like him.

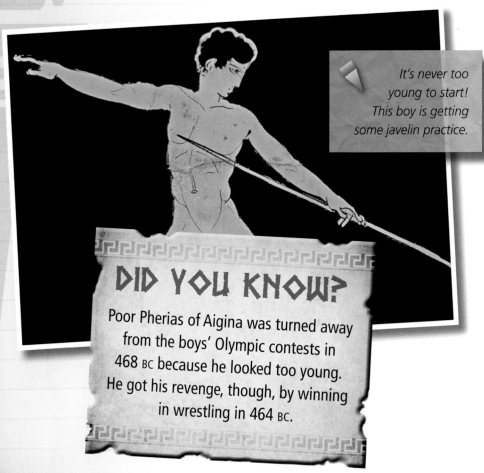

It's never too young to start! This boy is getting some javelin practice.

DID YOU KNOW?

Poor Pherias of Aigina was turned away from the boys' Olympic contests in 468 BC because he looked too young. He got his revenge, though, by winning in wrestling in 464 BC.

It's a hard slog!

Becoming a sports hero means lots of hard work and dedication. It means working with a trainer, special diets, getting up at dawn, and long days of fitness and practice. You will have to win minor competitions before being invited to the big Games.

It's definitely going to be tough. But if you're good enough, it will be worth it. And, what do you know? I happen to have a few places left at my training school! When can you start?

They probably can't punch very hard yet, but these young boys show plenty of promise!

THE YOUNGEST (BOYS') CHAMPION

The youngest ever winner in the boys' Olympic competition was Damascos of Messene. He won the *stadion* race when he was just 12.

GLOSSARY

barbarian Uncivilized person

choke hold Fighting move that strangles your opponent

citizen Person who lives in a place and is allowed to vote there

city-state A small country with just one city in it

dignitary Person of high rank

equestrian Relating to horse-based sports

massage Muscle rub for relaxation

minae Greek money

modest Not emphasizing one's own abilities

mortal Human; subject to death

pankration A combat sport that combined boxing and wrestling

pentathlete Athlete that competed in five contests in one event

prosecuted Put on trial

rival Competitor

sacrificed Killed as part of a religious ceremony

spectator Someone who watches an event

taverna Place where people eat and drink

wreath circle of leaves for winners of competitions

Olympic Sports

Running Events

The first two events are sprint races. The second two are for athletes with good endurance and strength.
- *stadion* (one length of the track)
- *diaulos* (twice as far as the *stadion*)
- *dolichos* (about ten times as far as the *diaulos*)
- race-in-armor (*diaulos* distance, but wearing only armor!)

Pentathlon

- The "five contests" of pentathlon are long jump, discus, javelin, running, and wrestling. You need to be fit, strong, and fast for the pentathlon.

Combat Sports

You need to be big and strong, not mind being hit, and be able to react quickly.
- wrestling
- boxing
- *pankration*

Equestrian

Unless you're rich, you can ignore this event! Only the rich can afford to keep horses and bring them to the Games. Horse races take place on a large, flat area called a *hippodrome*.
- four-horse chariot
- two-horse chariot
- horse with rider

FURTHER INFORMATION

You can find out more about the world Adrastos lived in from a variety of sources.

Web sites

This excellent Web site from Tufts University in the United States is filled with material about the ancient Olympics. The sections on Athletes' Stories and A Tour of Ancient Olympia are especially good. Find them at:
www.perseus.tufts.edu/Olympics/

This Web site from the University of Leuven in Belgium contains an especially good annotated map of the Olympic site. Click on "Olympia," then on the word "map" at:
http://ancientolympics.arts.kuleuven.be/index.html

Books

I wonder Why Greeks Built Temples? And Other Questions About Ancient Greece by Fiona Macdonald. Kingfisher Books (2006).

How to Be an Ancient Greek Athlete by Jacqueline Morley. National Geographic Children's Books (2008).

Ancient Olympic Games (The Olympics) by Haydn Middleton. Heinemann Library (2007).

Life in Ancient Greece (Peoples of the Ancient World) by Lynn Peppas. Crabtree Publishing Company (2005).

INDEX